Introduction to Bookkeeping
Wise Guide

AAT Level 2 Certificate in Accounting

© Michael Fardon, I

All rights reserved. No part of this publication may be reproduced, stored in a retrieval system form or by any means, electronic, mechanical, photo-copying, recording or otherwise, without t copyright owners, or in accordance with the provisions of the Copyright, Designs and Patents / terms of any licence permitting limited copying issued by the Copyright Licensing Agency, Saff Street, London EC1N 8TS.

Image of owl © Eric Isselée-Fotolia.com

Published by Osborne Books Limited, Printed and bound by Stroma Ltd, UK.

Email books@osbornebooks.co.uk, Website www.osbornebooks.co.uk

ISBN 978-1-911198-84-0

how to use this Wise Guide

This Wise Guide has been designed to supplement your Tutorial and Workbook. It has two main aims:

- to reinforce your learning as you study your course
- to help you prepare for your online assessment

This Wise Guide is organised in the specific topic areas listed on pages 4 and 5. These individual topic areas have been designed to cover the main areas of study, concentrating on specific areas of difficulty. There is also an index at the back to help you find the areas you are studying or revising.

The Owl symbolises wisdom, and acts as your tutor, introducing and explaining topics. Please let us know if he is doing his job properly. If you have feedback on this material, please email books@osbornebooks.co.uk.

Thank you and good luck with your study and revision.

Osborne Books

REVISION TIPS

*'OWL' stands for: **O**bserve **W**rite **L**earn*

There are a number of well-known ways in which you can remember information:

- *You can remember what it looks like on the page. Diagrams, lists, mind-maps, colour coding for different types of information, all help you **observe** and remember.*

- *You can remember what you **write** down. Flash cards, post-it notes around the bathroom mirror, notes on a mobile phone all help. It is the process of writing which fixes the information in the brain.*

- *You can **learn** by using this Wise Guide. Read through each topic carefully and then prepare your own written version on flash cards, post-it notes, wall charts – anything that you can see regularly.*

- *Lastly, give yourself **chill out** time, your brain a chance to recover and the information time to sink in. Promise yourself treats when you have finished studying – a drink, chocolate, a work out. Relax! And pass.*

list of contents

1	The accounting process	6
2	Double-entry	8
3	The accounting equation	14
4	Capital and revenue	20
5	Balancing accounts	23
6	Financial documents	27
7	Financial documents – the details	36
8	Discounts and VAT	38
9	Documents to day books	44
10	Sales day books to ledger accounts	49
11	Purchases day books to ledger accounts	52

12	Prompt payment discounts account postings	55
13	Reconciling supplier and customer accounts	57
14	Cash book – introduction	62
15	Balancing the cash book	68
16	Cash book to ledger accounts	74
17	Petty cash book	80
18	Petty cash book to ledger accounts	90
19	The trial balance	94
20	Digital bookkeeping	98
21	Memory aids	100
	Index	104

1 The accounting process

THE ACCOUNTING PROCESS

This process involves the recording of financial transactions, based on information taken from financial documents, eg invoices, credit notes. The process records transactions such as:
- *purchases*
- *sales*
- *payment of expenses*

this process follows a number of steps . . .

▨ the document is first recorded in a book of prime entry, eg a day book

▨ the data is then entered in ledger (double-entry) accounts

▨ and is summarised in a list of accounts – the trial balance – which provides owners and management with financial information

the accounting process

FINANCIAL TRANSACTIONS	a sale, a purchase, a payment
FINANCIAL DOCUMENTS	an invoice, a credit note, a remittance advice
BOOKS OF PRIME ENTRY	where the document is first recorded in the books, eg a day book
DOUBLE-ENTRY ACCOUNTS	double-entry ledger accounts
TRIAL BALANCE	a listing of the ledger accounts

2   Double-entry

THE DOUBLE-ENTRY SYSTEM

This can be a pain to get to grips with in the first place as it seems very complicated, with so many things to remember. But once you have got it worked out, it is very straightforward.

So remember:

- For every transaction, there are entries in **two accounts**.
- Each account has two sides:
  - a **debit** (often written as **dr**) side on the **left** (UK drivers **dr**ive on the **left**)
  - a **credit** (often written as **cr**) side on the **right** (UK drivers **cr**ash on the **right**)
- The accounts are often set out in the form of a 'T' with the account name at the top.
- Each transaction has a debit entry in one account and a credit entry in the other account, as shown on the next page.

debit (dr)	Account name	credit (cr)
debit entry		

debit (dr)	Account name	credit (cr)
		credit entry

EXAMPLE
Buying a **computer** for £3,000 and paying by electronic transfer from the **bank**.

debit (dr)	Computer Account	credit (cr)
Bank	3,000	

debit (dr)	Bank Account	credit (cr)
	Computer	3,000

introduction to bookkeeping wise guide – double-entry

EXAMPLE

Receiving £5,000 cash from **sales** and paying it into the **bank**.

debit (dr)	Sales Account		credit (cr)
		Bank	5,000

debit (dr)	Bank Account		credit (cr)
Sales	5,000		

RULES OF DOUBLE-ENTRY

- For every transaction, there are entries in two accounts.

- For every transaction, there is one debit entry and one credit entry.

- In the case of the bank account, the entries can be either debit or credit.

- The name included in each entry is the name of the other account.

should the account have a debit entry or a credit entry?

This is the big problem.

It becomes easy once you have learnt the basic rules that state which type of account normally has debit entries and which type of account has credit entries.

There are various ways in which you can do this, and when learning about double-entry you should be guided by your tutor.

When you have got a good grasp of debits and credits, you may find it useful to use the 'Memory aids' Section on page 100.

One useful method of learning the rules is to memorise this chart.

debit (dr)	credit (cr)
Purchases	Revenue
Expenses	Liabilities and Capital
Assets	Sales

more detail about debits (left-hand side)

debit (dr)	credit (cr)
Purchases	Revenue
Expenses	Liabilities - items owed and Capital
Assets	Sales

■ **Purchases**
Purchases in this case are purchases of goods which a business sells.

■ **Expenses**
These are the running expenses (costs) of a business – wages, for example.

■ **Assets**
Assets are items that a business **owns**: vehicles, computers, money in the bank.
Another asset is money **owed to** a business by customers (receivables).

All these items will appear as **debits** – on the left-hand side of the double-entry accounts.

more detail about credits (right-hand side)

debit (dr)	**credit (cr)**
Purchases	Revenue
Expenses	Liabilities - items owed and Capital
Assets	Sales

- **Revenue**
  Revenue is the term used for the income items of a business, for example rent received from letting out an office.

- **Liabilities**
  These are items a business owes, for example bank loans and money to suppliers (payables). It also includes **Capital**, the money put in by the owner(s).

- **Sales**
  This is the money received from the sales of products or services.

All these items will appear as **credits** – on the right-hand side.

introduction to bookkeeping wise guide – double-entry

3 The accounting equation

ASSETS – LIABILITIES = CAPITAL

*The principle which underlies double-entry bookkeeping is the **accounting equation**.*

When you understand this principle, the way in which double-entry works will become much clearer.

starting a business

If you start a business, you will have a shopping list for things you will need to get hold of. These are **assets**. But you will need to provide money for all this:

- with your own money; this is **capital** – the owner's investment and profits

- you can borrow money and buy on credit; these are **liabilities** – items that you owe

The **accounting equation** is just common sense:

what you buy and what you own **minus** what you have borrowed and owe **equals capital**, ie what your business is worth to you or to anyone who might want to buy it

This can be put another way: **assets – liabilities = capital**

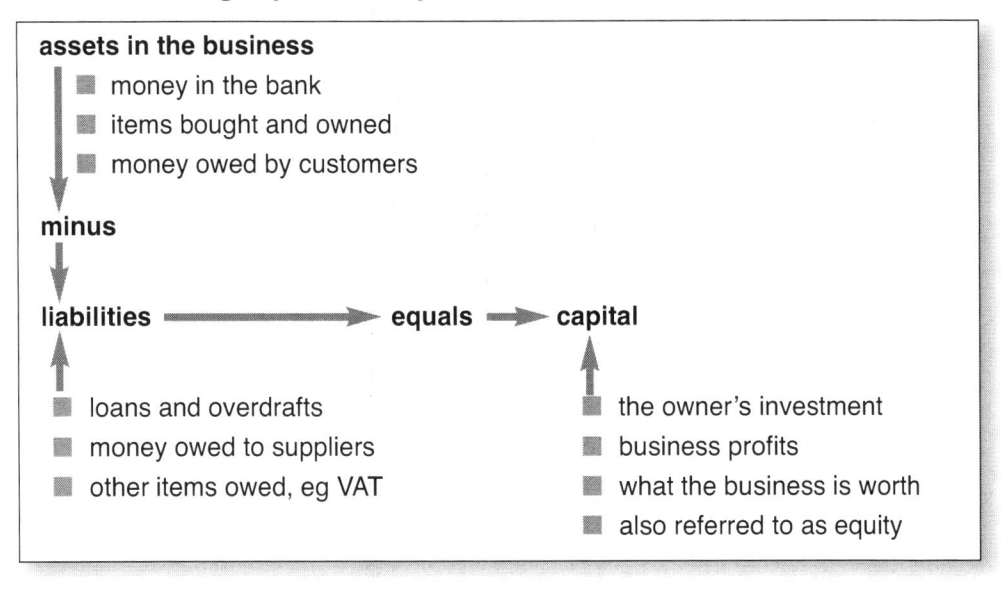

the accounting equation explained

assets in the business
- money in the bank
- items bought and owned
- money owed by customers

minus

liabilities ⟶ **equals** ⟶ **capital**

- loans and overdrafts
- money owed to suppliers
- other items owed, eg VAT

- the owner's investment
- business profits
- what the business is worth
- also referred to as equity

the accounting equation and double-entry – so what?

You may well ask what the accounting equation has to do with double-entry. Read through the two pages that follow – you will see that as time passes and financial transactions are made, the double-entry that you carry out ensures that the accounting equation always balances exactly.

RULES FOR DOUBLE-ENTRY TRANSACTIONS

First of all you will need to remember how changes in assets, capital and liabilities are recorded in the double-entry system:

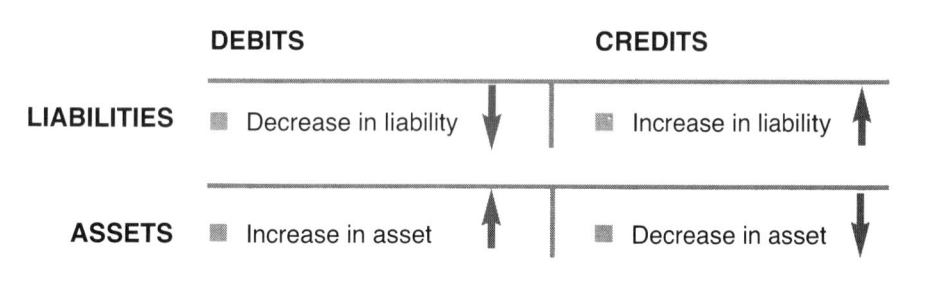

	DEBITS	CREDITS
LIABILITIES	Decrease in liability	Increase in liability
ASSETS	Increase in asset	Decrease in asset

Now you can apply these rules to some examples, as shown on the next few pages.

EXAMPLE

The owner invests £100,000 of capital in the business and pays it into the bank account.

The double-entry account entries are:

- debit bank account £100,000
- credit capital account £100,000

This means you are:

- increasing an asset (bank account) by £100,000 – a **debit**
- increasing capital (capital account) by £100,000 – a **credit**

so what is the effect on the accounting equation?

- The accounting equation still balances because all you have done is added the same amount of £100,000 to both sides:

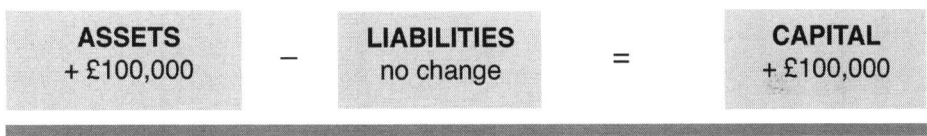

| **ASSETS** + £100,000 | − | **LIABILITIES** no change | = | **CAPITAL** + £100,000 |

introduction to bookkeeping wise guide – the accounting equation

EXAMPLE

The owner buys a **computer** for £15,000 and pays from the business **bank** account. The double-entry account entries are:

- **debit computer account** £15,000
- **credit bank account** £15,000

This means you are:

- increasing an asset (computer account) by £15,000 – a **debit**
- decreasing an asset (bank account) by £15,000 – a **credit**

so what is the effect on the accounting equation?

- There is no change to the accounting equation because all you have done is swapped one asset (money in the bank) for another (a computer).
- There is no change to either capital or liabilities.

ASSETS + £15,000 – £15,000 = no change	–	LIABILITIES no change	=	CAPITAL no change

EXAMPLE

The owner pays a **supplier** invoice for £2,000 from the business **bank** account.
The double-entry account entries are:

- **debit supplier account** £2,000
- **credit bank account** £2,000

This means you are:

- decreasing a liability (supplier account) by £2,000 – a **debit**
- decreasing an asset (bank account) by £2,000 – a **credit**

so what is the effect on the accounting equation?

- There is no change to the accounting equation because you have reduced both the assets and the liabilities by £2,000 so that the net figure will be the same.
- The accounting equation still balances.

ASSETS	–	LIABILITIES	=	CAPITAL
– £2,000		– £2,000		no change

introduction to bookkeeping wise guide – the accounting equation

4 Capital and revenue

CAPITAL OR REVENUE EXPENSE?

In accounting you need to understand the difference between:

- *Capital expense – payment for non-current (fixed) assets and the associated costs*

- *Revenue expense – day-to-day running expenses*

Remember!

- A **current asset** is something owned by the business for the short term, eg inventory, money in the bank.

- A **non-current (fixed) asset** is owned by the business for the long term, eg property, computers, vehicles.

Capital expense includes:

- the **purchase cost** of non-current assets such as property, machinery and computers – ie items which are kept for the long term
- the **installation cost** of non-current assets such as property and machinery
- the **cost of improvement** (but not repair) of non-current assets, eg extending a property
- the **legal cost** of purchasing non-current assets such as property

Revenue expense is the day-to-day cost of running the business; it includes:

- **purchases** of inventory which will be resold or used in manufacturing
- **selling expenses** such as advertising and distribution
- **administration expenses** such as wages, power bills and stationery
- **repair and maintenance** of non-current assets, for example decorating, cleaning

CAPITAL OR REVENUE INCOME?

*In accounting you will also come across **capital income** and **revenue income** and you will need to know the difference between the two types of income.*

Capital income includes:

- money received from the sale of non-current assets such as property

- bank loans received

- extra capital invested by the business owner

Revenue income includes:

- money received from sales

- regular amounts received, eg rent received, commission received, prompt payment discounts

5 Balancing accounts

WHY DO ACCOUNTS NEED BALANCING?

*Balancing an account means calculating the **up-to-date total amount** in any account at the end of a period, eg total sales, the bank balance, the total wages paid out. These figures are needed for **management** and also for setting up the **trial balance**.*

steps for calculating an account balance

Look at the customer account below and follow the numbered steps on the pages that follow to find out the customer's balance, ie how much Bella Catering owes.

Dr			Bella Catering		Cr
		£			£
1 Mar	Balance b/d	200	3 Mar	Bank	200
4 Mar	Sales	250	5 Mar	Sales returns	50
5 Mar	Sales	300			

introduction to bookkeeping wise guide – balancing accounts

Step 1 – total the debit and credit columns and work out the difference

- Add up the debit and credit columns to produce separate totals.

- Do not enter figures in ink in the account at this stage.

- You can write down the totals on a separate piece of paper – or pencil in the figures in the account as a temporary subtotal, as shown in grey here.

- Work out the difference between the two totals. This is the **balance**, the amount owed by Bella Catering. The calculation is: £750 – £250 = **£500**.

  You will need this total for the next step when you write this balance in the account.

Dr				Bella Catering	Cr
		£			£
1 Mar	Balance b/d	200	3 Mar	Bank	200
4 Mar	Sales	250	5 Mar	Sales returns	50
5 Mar	Sales	300		temporary totals can be pencilled in	
		750			250

Step 2 – enter the balance on the correct side and calculate the column totals

- Enter the balance you have worked out in Step 1 (£500).
  - on the side of the lower total (here it is the credit side)
  - on the next available line (rubbing out any pencilled subtotals first)
  - plus the date and the description 'Balance c/d' (or 'Balance carried down')

- Now total the debits and credits (the totals should be the same, in this case £750) and enter these totals on the same level. Put a single line above the totals and a double line or heavy line under the totals – this line means that nothing should be added to or subtracted from these figures.

Dr			**Bella Catering**		Cr
		£			£
1 Mar	Balance b/d	200	3 Mar	Bank	200
4 Mar	Sales	250	5 Mar	Sales returns	50
5 Mar	Sales	300	**5 Mar**	**Balance c/d**	**500**
		750			**750**

enter the balance you have calculated

total up both columns and check the totals are the same

introduction to bookkeeping wise guide – balancing accounts

Step 3 – complete the double entry by carrying down the balance

▨ Because you have entered £500 on the **credit** side of this double-entry account, you will also need to enter £500 on the **debit** side, but in the same account.

▨ This entry is made on the debit side on the next line **below** the totals of £750.

   – with the date of the next working day

   – with the description of 'Balance b/d' (or 'Balance brought down')

Remember!

'**C**arried down' or '**c**/d' is always the entry higher up, beginning with 'c' = **c**rown.

'**B**rought down' or '**b**/d' is always the entry below, beginning with 'b' = **b**ottom.

Dr			Bella Catering			Cr
		£				£
1 Mar	Balance b/d	200	3 Mar	Bank		200
4 Mar	Sales	250	5 Mar	Sales returns		50
5 Mar	Sales	300	5 Mar	**Balance c/d**		**500**
		750				750
6 Mar	**Balance b/d**	**500**				

the balance b/d is normally a day after the balance c/d

enter the balance you have calculated

6 Financial documents

Financial documents result from financial transactions and are the basis of many of the entries into the accounting system.

*When dealing with documents you need first to sort out whether you are the **seller** or the **buyer**, and also whether you are **issuing** or **receiving** the documents. A typical sales transaction (ignoring any returns or refunds) looks like this:*

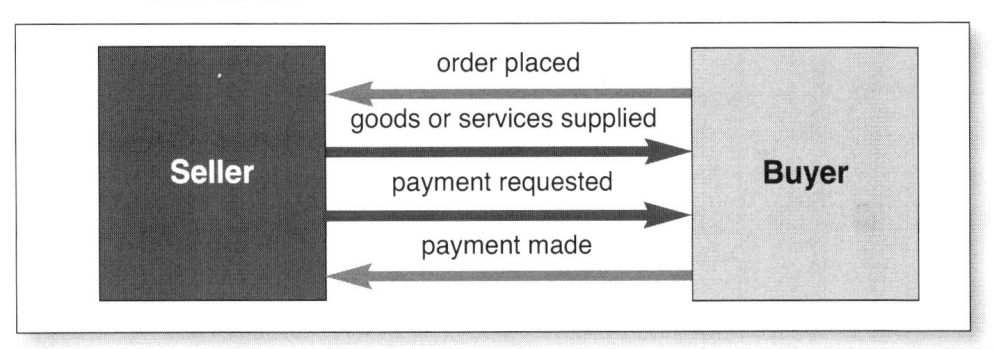

Seller		Buyer
	← order placed	
	goods or services supplied →	
	payment requested →	
	← payment made	

introduction to bookkeeping wise guide – financial documents

The MAIN FINANCIAL DOCUMENTS sent between the buyer and the seller are:

- **quotation** – sometimes the buyer may request a formal quotation for the goods or services required; this will provide the information used in the purchase order

- **purchase order** – the details of an order placed by a buyer, eg product code and the quantity of the goods required, price and reference to any bulk or trade discount normally given by the seller

- **delivery note** – details of the goods (or services) supplied and sent out by the seller with the goods

- **invoice** – this is sent by the seller; it sets out how much has to be paid, when and on what terms

- **goods returned note** – sent out by the buyer with any goods returned to the seller (eg faulty or incorrect goods)

- **credit note** – sent by the seller, reducing the amount owed by the buyer

- **statement of account** – sets out the amount owing by a buyer, sent out by the seller

- **remittance advice** – sent by the buyer, gives the seller the details of payment being made by the buyer

the flow of documents – the seller's point of view

This shows how various documents pass between the seller and the buyer at various stages in the transaction. It is set out from the **seller's** point of view.

Seller → / ← Buyer	
→	**quotation** sent by the seller to the buyer on request
←	**purchase order** received from buyer
→	**delivery note** sent with the goods
→	**invoice** sent to buyer requesting payment
←	**goods returned note** sent by buyer *if* goods are returned
→	**credit note** sent by seller *if* goods are returned or refund is due for any other reason
→	**statement of account** sent to buyer stating what is due
←	**remittance advice** sent by buyer stating what is being paid

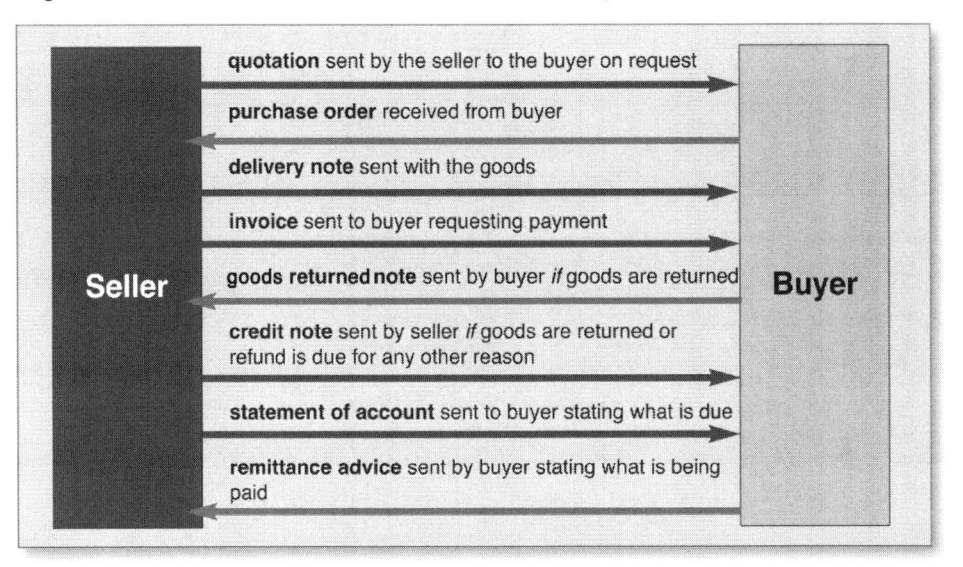

the flow of documents – the buyer's point of view

This shows how various documents pass between the buyer and the seller at various stages in the transaction. It is set out from the **buyer's** point of view.

Buyer		Seller
	← **quotation** sent by the seller to the buyer on request	
	purchase order sent to seller →	
	← **delivery note** received with the goods	
	← **invoice** received by buyer requesting payment	
	goods returned note sent by buyer *if* goods are returned →	
	← **credit note** received by buyer *if* goods are returned or refund is due for any other reason	
	← **statement of account** received by buyer stating what is due	
	remittance advice sent by buyer stating what is being paid →	

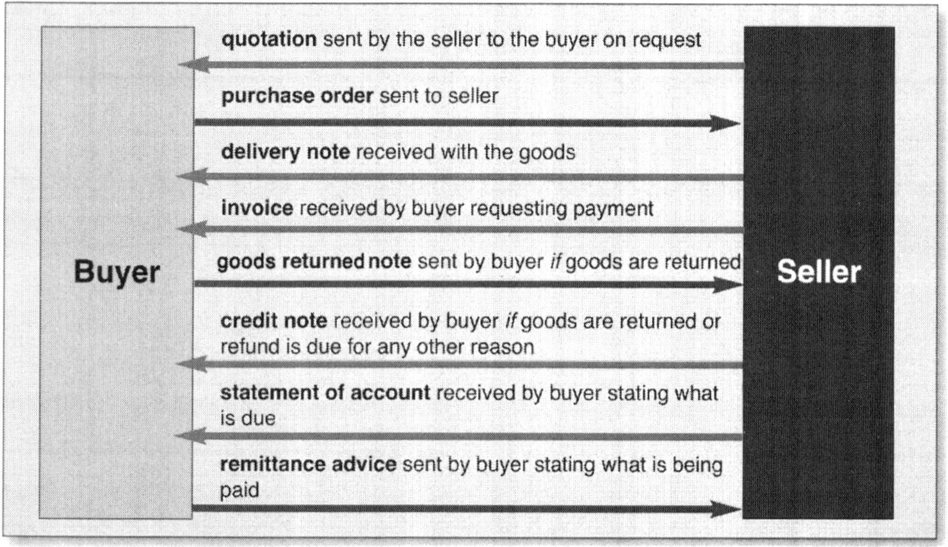

the invoice – setting out the payment due

Not all invoices are set out in exactly the same way, but they will all normally contain the same information. The details to be entered are indicated below.

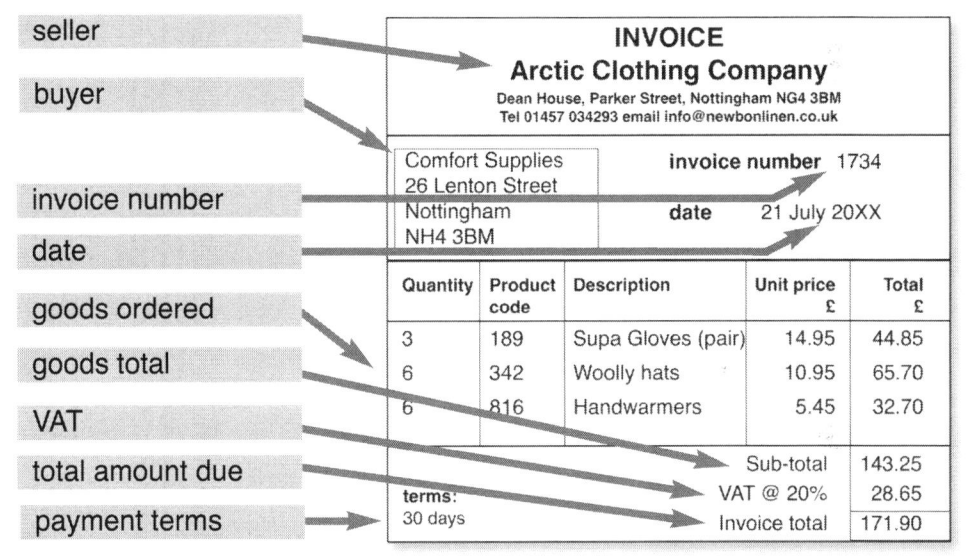

INVOICE

Arctic Clothing Company

Dean House, Parker Street, Nottingham NG4 3BM
Tel 01457 034293 email info@newbonlinen.co.uk

- **seller**
- **buyer**: Comfort Supplies, 26 Lenton Street, Nottingham, NH4 3BM
- **invoice number**: 1734
- **date**: 21 July 20XX

Quantity	Product code	Description	Unit price £	Total £
3	189	Supa Gloves (pair)	14.95	44.85
6	342	Woolly hats	10.95	65.70
6	816	Handwarmers	5.45	32.70
			Sub-total	143.25
			VAT @ 20%	28.65
			Invoice total	171.90

terms: 30 days

- goods ordered
- goods total
- VAT
- total amount due
- payment terms

credit note – setting out a reduction in the amount due

Credit notes are 'refund' documents set out in a very similar format to the invoice. They indicate to the buyer the reduction that will be made to the amount owing.

seller	**CREDIT NOTE** **Arctic Clothing Company** Dean House, Parker Street, Nottingham NG4 3BM Tel 01457 034293 email info@newbonlinen.co.uk
buyer	Comfort Supplies 26 Lenton Street Nottingham NH4 3BM
credit note number	credit note number 634
date	date 31 July 20XX

Quantity	Product code	Description	Unit price £	Total £
1	612	Sheepskin hat	24.00	24.00

reason for return: faulty goods

Sub-total	24.00
VAT @ 20%	4.80
Credit note total	28.80

- details of faulty goods returned
- reason for return
- total refund due, with VAT shown

statement of account – showing the amount due and for what

A statement of account is sent out to a customer who buys on credit, setting out:

- details of entries to the customer account (with appropriate reference numbers)
- amounts invoiced (debit column)
- payments received and credit notes received (credit column)
- a running total of the account (balance column) including the total amount owed

STATEMENT OF ACCOUNT			FROM **Vogue Limited** 56 Shaftesbury Road Manorfield MA1 6GP	
TO Ditzy Dames 67 Martley Road Borchester BO1 9BC				
date	details	debit (£)	credit (£)	balance (£)
01 03 20XX	Balance b/f	250.00		250.00
02 03 20XX	Payment received		220.00	30.00
02 03 20XX	Invoice 78254	890.50		920.50
10 03 20XX	Credit note 12157		44.00	876.50
			TOTAL DUE	**876.50**

remittance advice – notification of a payment made and what it covers

A remittance advice is sent to the seller by a credit customer, indicating what is being paid in settlement of an account and **how**. The remittance advice sets out:

- the date, amount and invoice number for invoices included in the payment
- the date, amount and credit note number for credit notes deducted from the payment (the amount may be shown in brackets as it is a 'minus' amount)
- the total payment amount and the means of payment, eg 'cheque' or 'BACS'

REMITTANCE ADVICE

TO	FROM
Molto di Moda 45 Floral Street London N19 6GH	**Vogue Limited** **56 Shaftesbury Road** **Manorfield** **MA1 6GP**
9 July 20XX	

date	your reference	our reference	payment amount
03 06 XX	INVOICE 787213	876225	460.00
15 06 XX	CREDIT NOTE 12088	876225	(92.00)
	BACS PAYMENT TOTAL		368.00

a note on coding

Coding means giving something a unique series of letters and/or numbers which will identify that 'something'. Common examples are car registration plates, postcodes, National Insurance numbers, flight numbers, online catalogue numbers.

In a business context, unique codes are used to identify documents such as purchase orders, invoices, credit notes and inventory items.

There are various systems of coding which can be used:

- **alphabetical** – using just letters, eg 'ABC'
- **numerical** – using just numbers, normally in sequence, eg '217845'
- **alphanumerical** – using letters and numbers, eg 'FAB1236'

Common examples of coding in accounting include:

- **numerical** – invoice and credit note numbers, ledger account numbers
- **alphanumerical** – product codes, credit customer or supplier account codes (which can start with the first letters of the customer name), eg 'CAM207'

Checking of coding is essential when documents need to 'match up' in the accounting system, eg an order reference with an invoice and statement.

7   Financial documents – the details

THE INVOICE – THE NEED FOR ACCURATE DETAILS

There is no 'right' or 'wrong' format for an invoice, but there must be certain basic details given which will enable the correct calculation to take place. These are shown in the format on the next page.

These details include:

- **quantity** – the number of items (taken from the purchase order)

- **code** – the inventory or catalogue code of the product (taken from the purchase order)

- **description** – what the product is, eg a computer, an hour charged for bookkeeping services

- **amount** – the total price before VAT is added on and after the deduction of discount (the 'net' price)

- **VAT** – the amount charged for VAT (Value Added Tax)

- **total** – the price after VAT has been added on (the 'gross' amount)

an invoice calculation

This example is just one way in which the calculations on an invoice or credit note may be set out. You will encounter many different formats in practice. The important point is that all the details listed on the previous page must be present in one form or another so that the calculations can be seen and checked.

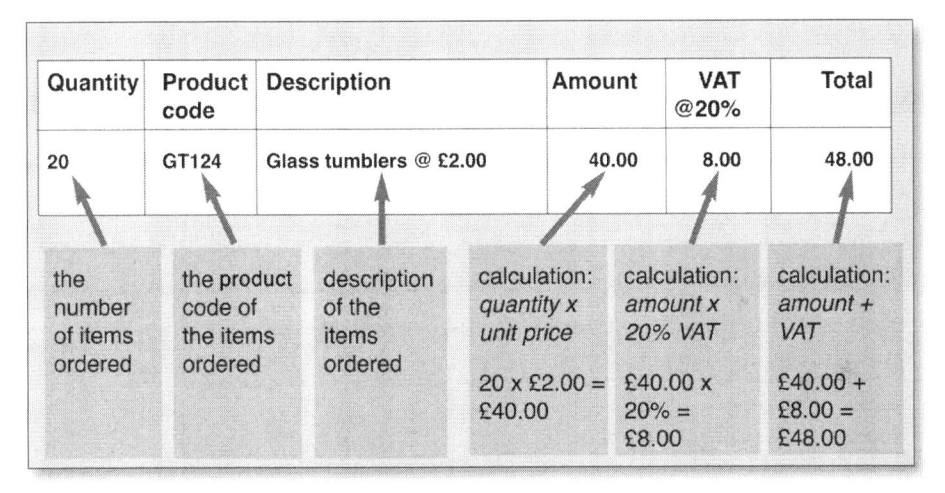

Quantity	Product code	Description	Amount	VAT @20%	Total
20	GT124	Glass tumblers @ £2.00	40.00	8.00	48.00

| the number of items ordered | the product code of the items ordered | description of the items ordered | calculation: *quantity x unit price*

 20 x £2.00 = £40.00 | calculation: *amount x 20% VAT*

 £40.00 x 20% = £8.00 | calculation: *amount + VAT*

 £40.00 + £8.00 = £48.00 |

introduction to bookkeeping wise guide – financial documents - the details

8 Discounts and VAT

CALCULATING DISCOUNTS

Calculating discounts can sometimes be a problem.

But, as with many problem areas in accounting, discounts can be sorted out by remembering a series of defined steps.

You will first need to remember the types of discount:

- **trade discount** – a percentage reduction in the selling price given by sellers to established customers, normally businesses (ie 'in the trade') rather than the general public

- **bulk discount** – a percentage reduction in the selling price given by sellers to customers who buy large quantities; the percentage sometimes increases in line with the quantity supplied

These two types of discount are shown on invoices and credit notes but **not in the accounting records**.

- **prompt payment discount** (also known as **cash discount** and **settlement discount**) – a reduction in the selling price of goods which can be received by the customer when payment is made promptly, eg 'within 7 days'

  This discount is **optional**, and is **recorded in the accounting records** as an expense to the seller.

calculation of trade and bulk discount

Trade and **bulk** discount are more straightforward. They are a standard percentage deduction from the selling price, as shown below and illustrated on the next page.

EXAMPLE

Glass tumblers which cost £2 each before discount or VAT are sold with a 20% trade discount given to the buyer. The calculation is:

1	Calculate the price **before** discount	100 x £2	=	£200
2	Calculate the **20%** trade discount on £200	£200 x $\frac{20}{100}$	=	£40
3	Calculate the price **after** deducting discount	£200 – £40	=	£160

Quantity	Product code	Description	Total	Discount @20%	Net total
100	GT124	Glass tumblers @ £2.00	200.00	40.00	160.00

calculation: 100 x £2.00 = £200.00 minus 20% discount (£40) = £160.

Note: the invoice extract shown above does not include the VAT calculation which continues to the right of the discount calculation. This is shown on the next page.

- The total after the deduction of discount is known as the **net total** and is shown on the extract from the invoice above in the right-hand column.

- The same process will be carried out if the discount is 'bulk' discount.

- The invoice extract above shows the calculations up to and including the deduction of the trade discount. The invoice will then go on to calculate and add on any VAT that will need to be charged. This is illustrated on the page below.

calculation of VAT

A **sales tax** – **VAT** (Value Added Tax in the UK) – is **added** to the net total on an invoice or credit note after any trade or bulk discount has been deducted.

EXAMPLE

This continues the calculation on the invoice shown on the previous page.

1. Calculate the **20**% VAT on the £160 net total and enter the figure in the VAT column   £160 × **20**/100 = £32

2. Add the **£32 VAT to** the £160 and enter the £192 in the Total column   £160 + **£32** = £192

The customer will be charged £192. The calculation will look like this on the invoice:

Previous columns: Quantity + Product code + Description	Total	Discount @20%	Net total	VAT @20%	Total
	200.00	40.00	160.00	32.00	192.00

introduction to bookkeeping wise guide – discounts and VAT

some notes on VAT and rounding

formula for working out the VAT on a given (net) amount

amount x $\frac{\text{VAT rate}}{100}$ = VAT to be charged

example: £120 x $\frac{20}{100}$ = £24 (to be added on to the £120 = £144)

calculating the VAT at a given rate included in a whole (gross) amount (eg £144)

▓ **Method 1** (VAT fraction of $^1/_6{}^*$): if VAT is 20%, divide the whole amount by 6.
example: £144 ÷ 6 = VAT of £24

* the VAT fraction is published by HMRC at www.hmrc.gov.uk

▓ **Method 2** (which is far more complicated):
$\frac{\text{VAT percentage (20)} \times \text{whole amount including VAT (£144)}}{\text{100 + VAT percentage (ie 100 + 20)}}$ = VAT of £24

'rounding' in calculations

▓ With **normal** calculations you should round **up or down** to the nearest figure.
▓ When calculating **VAT** you should **normally** round **down** to the nearest figure.
▓ Use the number of decimal places specified (it is often two decimal places).

prompt payment discount

Prompt payment discount is also known as 'cash discount' and 'settlement discount'. It is an optional discount which is available to the customer when payment of an invoice is made promptly according to terms set out on the invoice, eg 'within 15 days'.

how it works – an example

The normal method used (and the method examined by AAT in its assessments) is as follows:

- A VAT invoice issued by the seller for £200 will include in its terms (normally found at the bottom of the document) a statement such as *'5% prompt payment discount for settlement within 15 days'* – which in this case will be 5% of £200, ie £10.
- If the customer decides to pay **later than 15 days**, the amount paid to the seller will be the final invoice total (including the VAT charged at standard rate), ie £200.
- If the customer decides to pay **within 15 days**, the amount paid to the seller will be the final total less the prompt payment discount of 5%, ie £200 minus £10 = £190.
- If the discount is taken, the seller will then issue to the customer a credit note for the total amount of the prompt payment discount given, ie £10. This £10 includes both the goods amount and also the VAT.

9 Documents to day books

DAY BOOKS AND THE ACCOUNTING SYSTEM – AN OVERVIEW

The day books are summaries of financial transactions and form a vital link between financial documents (invoices and credit notes) and the double-entry ledger accounts.

what is a day book?

A day book is a **summary list of financial transactions, compiled from invoices or credit notes**. It enables a business to transfer a summary of sales and purchases transactions to the double-entry ledger accounts from a whole 'day' (or other set period) rather than one-by-one, which could prove complicated and time-consuming.

Day books are known as books of **prime entry**. As well as day books, there are other books of prime entry in the accounting system including **cash book** and **petty cash book**. As with the day books, these books of prime entry are used as a 'first stop' summary to record financial transactions which are then entered in the accounts.

sales, purchases and discounts day books

Sales, purchases and discount day books summarise information extracted from:

- invoices and credit notes **issued** to customers – **sales documents**
- invoices and credit notes **received** from suppliers – **purchases documents**

sales day book	compiled from **sales invoices** issued
sales returns day book	compiled from **sales credit notes** issued
discounts allowed day book	compiled from **sales credit notes** issued

purchases day book	compiled from **purchases invoices** received
purchases returns day book	compiled from **purchases credit notes** received
discounts received day book	compiled from **purchases credit notes** received

Note that if a prompt payment discount is taken, a credit note for the discount amount is issued by the seller and will be recorded in the seller's **discounts allowed** day book – and also in the buyer's **discounts received** day book. The next page shows how all these day books fit into the accounting system.

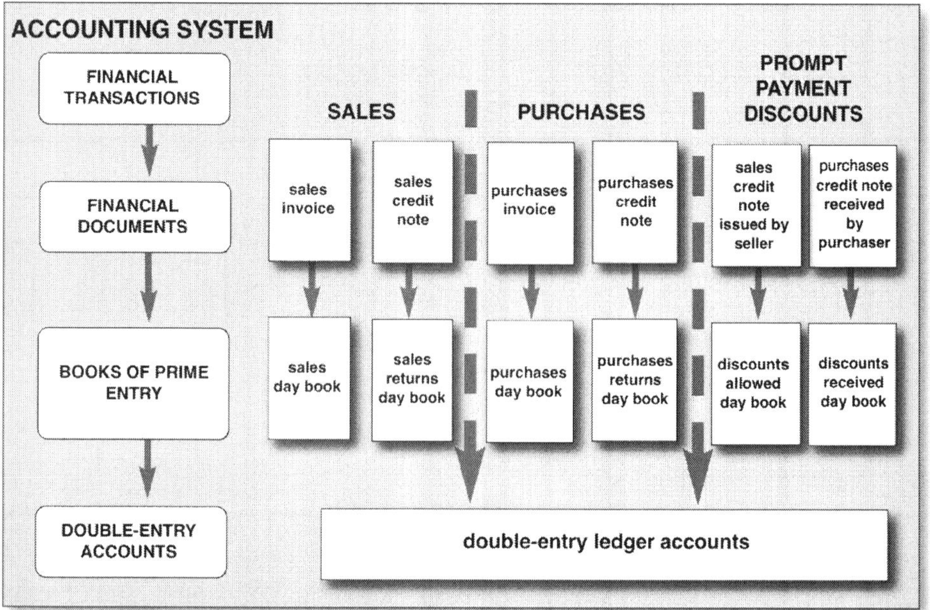

ACCOUNTING SYSTEM

					PROMPT PAYMENT DISCOUNTS
FINANCIAL TRANSACTIONS	**SALES**		**PURCHASES**		
↓					
FINANCIAL DOCUMENTS	sales invoice	sales credit note	purchases invoice	purchases credit note	sales credit note issued by seller / purchases credit note received by purchaser
↓	↓	↓	↓	↓	↓
BOOKS OF PRIME ENTRY	sales day book	sales returns day book	purchases day book	purchases returns day book	discounts allowed day book / discounts received day book
↓					
DOUBLE-ENTRY ACCOUNTS	double-entry ledger accounts				

format of day books

There is no set format for day books. The example format shown below is commonly used. The details entered in the various columns are taken from each individual sales invoice. The same procedure is followed for the other day books using the appropriate invoice or credit note. Day books can include analysis columns to identify separate products or product groups.

EXAMPLE: SALES DAY BOOK

Date 20XX	Details	Invoice Number	Total	VAT	Net
5 Aug	AB Supplies	19381	96.00	16.00	80.00
6 Aug	S Gerrard Limited	19382	144.00	24.00	120.00
7 Aug	Hermes Sports	19383	240.00	40.00	200.00

- the date of the invoice issued
- the name of the customer
- the invoice number
- the invoice total **after** VAT has been added on
- the VAT total from the invoice
- the invoice total **before** VAT has been added on

totalling the day books

The money columns of each day book must be totalled from time to time and it is these totals that will be transferred to various double-entry accounts in the appropriate ledgers. The totalling process is explained in the boxes below.

EXAMPLE: TOTALLED SALES DAY BOOK

Date 20XX	Details	Invoice Number	Total	VAT	Net
5 Aug	AB Supplies	19381	96.00	16.00	80.00
6 Aug	S Gerrard Limited	19382	144.00	24.00	120.00
7 Aug	Hermes Sports	19383	240.00	40.00	200.00
8 Aug			480.00	80.00	400.00

enter the date on which the day book is totalled

The 'Total', 'VAT' and 'Net' columns are all totalled.
The arithmetic is checked by adding the 'Net' and 'VAT' column totals. The result should equal the 'Total' column. In this case: £400 + £80 = £480

NEXT STEP – WRITING UP THE LEDGER ACCOUNTS

After the day books have been completed, the next step is the periodic transfer of the day book entries to the double-entry ledger accounts.

*We will first deal with the **sales day book** and the **sales returns day book**.*

which ledgers?

The two ledgers that will be used are the **receivables ledger** and the **general ledger**. On the next two pages you can see how the figures are transferred to the accounts.

RECEIVABLES LEDGER	GENERAL LEDGER
■ individual **customer accounts** showing entries for: – credit sales – credit sales returns	■ **receivables ledger control account** (total of credit customer accounts) ■ **sales account** (total of sales) ■ **sales returns account** (total of returns) ■ **VAT account** (VAT received)

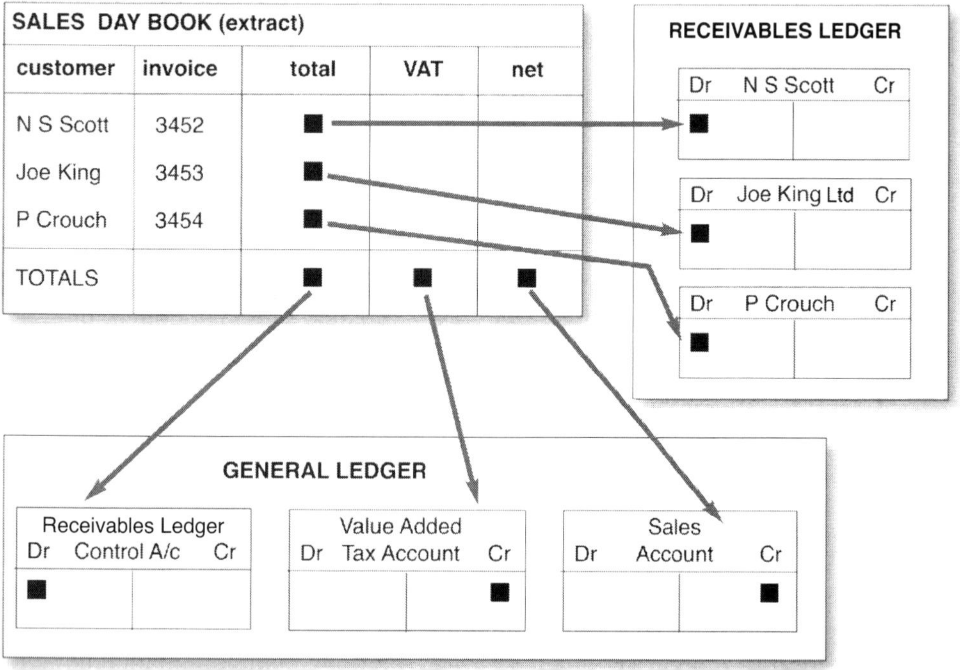

SALES DAY BOOK (extract)

customer	invoice	total	VAT	net
N S Scott	3452	■		
Joe King	3453	■		
P Crouch	3454	■		
TOTALS		■	■	■

RECEIVABLES LEDGER

Dr	N S Scott	Cr
■		

Dr	Joe King Ltd	Cr
■		

Dr	P Crouch	Cr
■		

GENERAL LEDGER

	Receivables Ledger	
Dr	Control A/c	Cr
■		

	Value Added	
Dr	Tax Account	Cr
		■

	Sales	
Dr	Account	Cr
		■

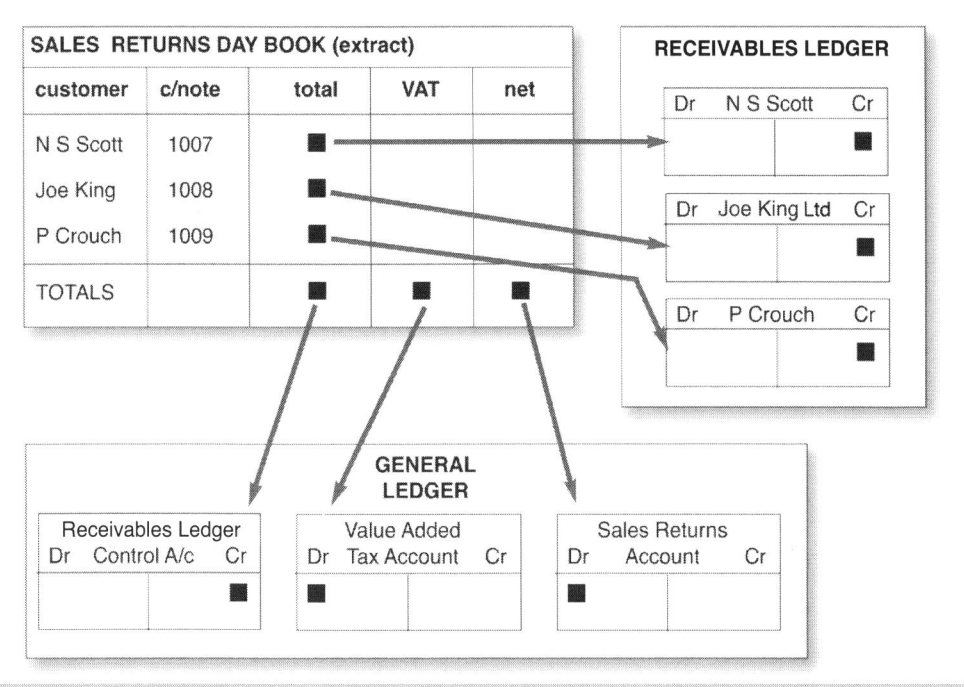

SALES RETURNS DAY BOOK (extract)

customer	c/note	total	VAT	net
N S Scott	1007	■		
Joe King	1008	■		
P Crouch	1009	■		
TOTALS		■	■	■

RECEIVABLES LEDGER

Dr   N S Scott   Cr

Dr   Joe King Ltd   Cr

Dr   P Crouch   Cr

GENERAL LEDGER

Receivables Ledger
Dr   Control A/c   Cr

Value Added
Dr   Tax Account   Cr

Sales Returns
Dr   Account   Cr

introduction to bookkeeping wise guide – sales day books to ledger accounts

11 Purchases day books to ledger accounts

PURCHASES: FROM DAY BOOKS TO DOUBLE-ENTRY ACCOUNTS

*Transfer of figures from the **purchases day book** and the **purchases returns day book** work in the same way as the transfers from the sales day books, except that supplier accounts relating to credit purchases are contained in the **payables ledger**.*

which ledgers?

The ledgers that will be used are the **payables ledger** and the **general ledger**.

On the next two pages you can see how the figures are transferred to the accounts.

PAYABLES LEDGER	GENERAL LEDGER

▨ individual **supplier accounts** showing entries for
    – credit purchases
    – credit purchases returns
	▨ **payables ledger control account** (total of credit supplier accounts)
	 ▨ **purchases account** (total purchases)
	 ▨ **purchases returns account** (total returns)
	 ▨ **VAT account** (VAT paid)

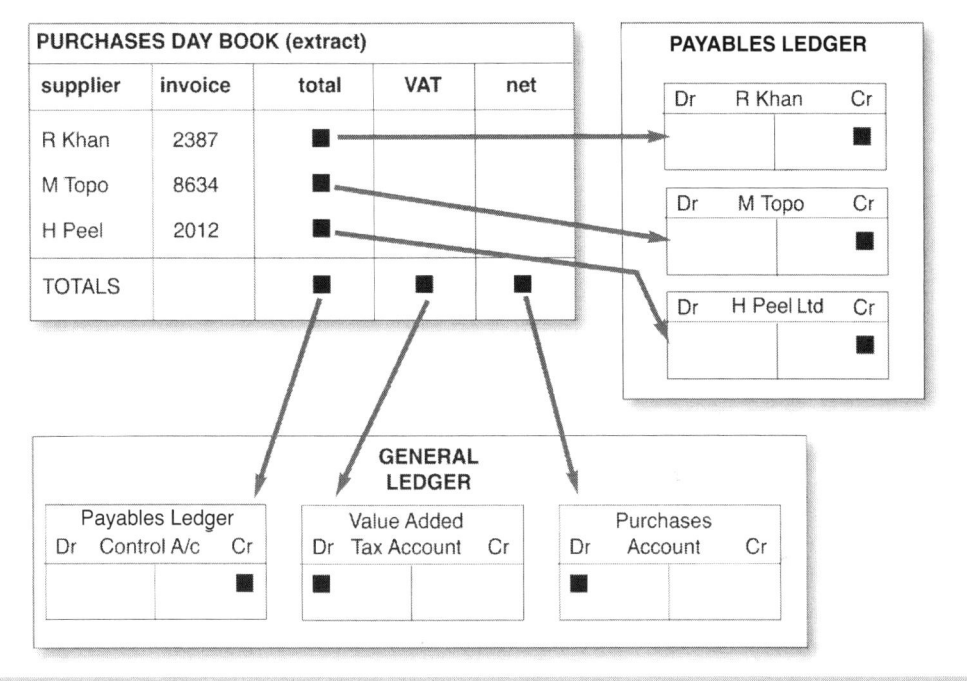

PURCHASES DAY BOOK (extract)

supplier	invoice	total	VAT	net
R Khan	2387	■		
M Topo	8634	■		
H Peel	2012	■		
TOTALS		■	■	■

PAYABLES LEDGER

Dr   R Khan   Cr

Dr   M Topo   Cr

Dr   H Peel Ltd   Cr

GENERAL LEDGER

Dr   Payables Ledger Control A/c   Cr

Dr   Value Added Tax Account   Cr

Dr   Purchases Account   Cr

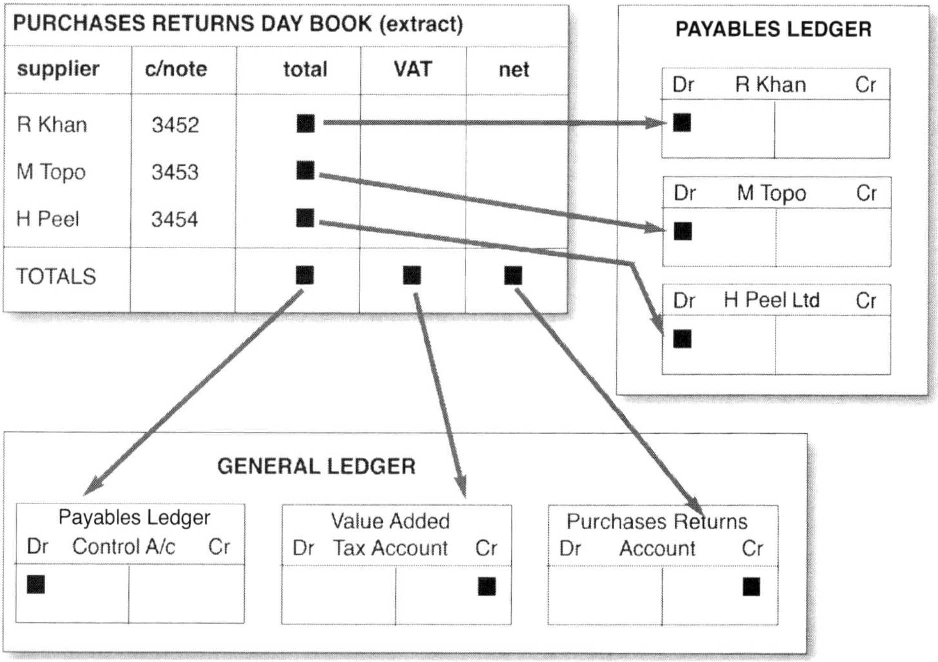

PURCHASES RETURNS DAY BOOK (extract)

supplier	c/note	total	VAT	net
R Khan	3452	■		
M Topo	3453	■		
H Peel	3454	■		
TOTALS		■	■	■

PAYABLES LEDGER

Dr	R Khan	Cr
■		

Dr	M Topo	Cr
■		

Dr	H Peel Ltd	Cr
■		

GENERAL LEDGER

	Payables Ledger	
Dr	Control A/c	Cr
■		

	Value Added	
Dr	Tax Account	Cr
		■

	Purchases Returns	
Dr	Account	Cr
		■

PROMPT PAYMENT DISCOUNTS – THE DAY BOOKS

Prompt payment discount, also known as **cash discount** and **settlement discount,** is an optional reduction in the total invoice amount which can be made by a purchaser when payment is made promptly, eg 'within 7 days'.

The problem from the bookkeeping point of view is that an invoice is issued, say for £120 (including VAT), but the purchaser deducts 5% (£6) of the invoice total and only pays £114. The invoice cannot be altered so the seller issues a credit note for £6 to the purchaser. The final amount due and paid is therefore £114 (ie £120 less £6).

This £6 reduction in the amount paid (including the VAT) will then be recorded in the day books of the seller and purchaser as follows:

Seller: discounts allowed day book: £6 entered from the credit note

Purchaser: discounts received day book: £6 entered from the credit note

This is illustrated on the next page. Remember that the £6 amounts involved include VAT.

Prompt payment discounts – posting to the ledgers – an example

Ibex Ltd sells goods to Trax Ltd for £120. Trax Ltd deducts a 5% prompt payment discount of £6 from the invoice total when making payment. Ibex Ltd then sends Trax Ltd a credit note for £6 which is entered in the day books and ledgers of Ibex Ltd and Trax Ltd as follows:

IBEX LTD – SELLER

Discounts allowed day book			
customer	total	VAT	net
Trax Ltd	6	1	5

Ledger entries – discounts allowed	
debit	
▪ discounts allowed account	£5
▪ VAT account	£1
credit	
▪ receivables ledger control account*	£6
* this control account entry will mirror the £6 entry in Trax Ltd's subsidiary receivables ledger account	

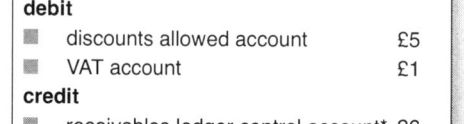

TRAX LTD – PURCHASER

Discounts received day book			
supplier	total	VAT	net
Ibex Ltd	6	1	5

Ledger entries – discounts received	
debit	
▪ payables ledger control account*	£6
credit	
▪ discounts received account	£5
▪ VAT account	£1
* this control account entry will mirror the £6 entry in Ibex Ltd's subsidiary payables ledger account	

13 Reconciling supplier and customer accounts

WHY DO SUPPLIER ACCOUNTS NEED RECONCILING?

If you order goods from a supplier on a regular basis on credit, you will receive a statement, often monthly, stating what they have invoiced and what you have paid and listing any returns and credit notes issued.

What if their statement and your account do not agree? You should always reconcile ('match up') the items on the supplier statement against the entries in the supplier account in your payables ledger.

what could cause a difference between the account and the statement?

- You have made payment but it does not yet show on the statement.
- A wrong amount is entered on the account or on the statement.
- An invoice or credit note is missing from either the statement or the account.
- An invoice shows on the statement, but you are disputing it, eg due to non-delivery, faulty or incomplete goods, or because of an overcharge.
- There is a duplicated transaction on the account or statement.

how to reconcile the difference

- Make sure the supplier's account in the payables ledger has been balanced.
- Tick off the items that are both in the supplier statement and the supplier's account in the payables ledger.
- If there is any item that is not ticked in either the statement or the account, this should account for the difference between the final balance of the statement and the balance brought down of the supplier's account.
- It can be useful to document this reconciliation by drawing up a document in the form of a statement, showing the difference and the reasons for the difference (eg payment from you not received by the supplier, or an invoice/credit note not received by you from the supplier). An example is shown below:

Reconciliation of supplier statement	
Balance on supplier statement	£512.60
Balance on supplier account in payables ledger	£361.20
Difference	£151.40
Reason for difference:	
Payment for £151.40 not yet received by supplier	

EXAMPLE

reconciling the statement with the supplier account in the payables ledger

SUPPLIER STATEMENT: BAXO IMPORTERS (extract)				
date	details	debit (£)	credit (£)	balance (£)
1 Nov 20XX	Balance b/d			✓ 650.00
5 Nov 20XX	BACS payment		✓ 650.00	00.00
19 Nov 20XX	Invoice 1902	✓ 850.00		850.00
26 Nov 20XX	Credit note 534		85.00	765.00
30 Nov 20XX	Total			765.00

item not in the supplier account (referring to the 85.00 credit note)

Dr	PAYABLES LEDGER: Baxo Importers					Cr
20XX			£	20XX		£
8 Nov	Bank		✓650.00	1 Nov	Balance b/d	✓650.00
30 Nov	Balance c/d		850.00	22 Nov	Purchases (Inv. 1902)	✓850.00
			1500.00			1500.00
				1 Dec	Balance b/d	850.00

introduction to bookkeeping wise guide – reconciling supplier statements

drawing up the account reconciliation

In the example shown on the previous page, note that:

- items in both the supplier statement and supplier account have been ticked off
- there is one item extra on the statement – a credit note for £85.00; this has not been ticked off
- this £85.00 represents the difference between the final balances of the supplier statement and the account, ie £85.00
- this is then recorded on the supplier reconciliation shown below:

Supplier statement reconciliation – Baxo Importers	
Balance on supplier statement	£765.00
Balance on supplier account in payables ledger	£850.00
Difference	− £85.00
Reason for difference: Credit note 534 for £85.00 not yet received from supplier	

Reconciling a supplier statement with the corresponding ledger account ensures that only accurate and timely payments are made. The potential for under- and over-payments is minimised, and all amounts, including discounts taken, will be correct.

reconciling payments from customers

A business that sells on credit should also make sure that payments received from customers reconcile (match up) with:

- the sales documents the business issues, eg invoices and credit notes
- previous payments received from the customer

A common practice is to reconcile each incoming payment against the details of the customer account in the receivables ledger.

The two documents that are frequently compared are:

- the **remittance advice** (if it includes details of what the payment covers)
- the latest customer **statement of account** (which will show all the transactions on the receivables ledger account)

If there is a difference between the amount due shown on the statement and the amount received, it should be calculated and traced to the relevant document(s).

14 Cash book – introduction

CASH BOOK – WHAT IT DOES

*The **cash book** records the money transactions of a business – money received and money paid out.*

*It is an important **book of prime entry** – ie the first place in which financial information is entered into the accounting system.*

The cash book records **money in** on the **left** and **money out** on the **right**.

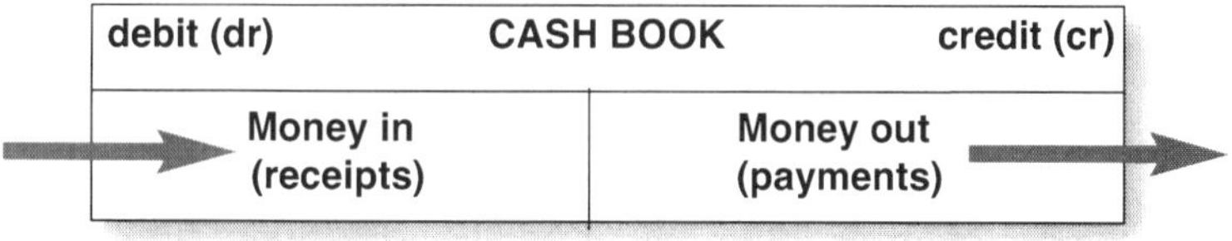

debit (dr)	CASH BOOK	credit (cr)
Money in (receipts)		Money out (payments)

The **cash book** incorporates two double-entry accounts which record:
- cash (notes and coins) received and paid out – this is **Cash account**
- incoming and outgoing bank transactions – this is **Bank account**

documents used:

Direct debit/standing order schedule; remittance advice; paying-in slip; cheque stub; cash receipt; receipts and payments listing; bank statement.

cash book entries – which side?

These are the main items that you will see entered in the cash book.

Look carefully at what goes on each side.

receipts (debits)	CASH BOOK	payments (credits)
■ receipts from cash sales to customers ■ receipts from credit customers (receivables) ■ other receipts, eg rent received		■ cash purchases from suppliers ■ payments to credit suppliers (payables) ■ other expenses, eg insurance

■ *When dealing with a '**cash**' customer or supplier, payment is made **straightaway**.*

■ *When dealing with a '**credit**' customer or supplier, payment is made **later**.*

money received – analysed cash book (debit side)

Cash books often include extra columns which **analyse** the amounts in the receipts and payments columns. In this system, each transaction is recorded **twice**, firstly in a **left-hand** column, and then **again** in the appropriate **right-hand** analysis column(s).

The columns of a debit side of a cash book are explained in the diagram below, and an example with sample entries is set out on the next page with explanatory notes.

CASH BOOK – debit side (receipts)				Analysis columns			
Date	Details	Cash	Bank	VAT	Cash sales	Receivables	Other income
		£	£	£	£	£	£
date of the entry	details of the entry	receipts		VAT	cash sales less VAT	receipts from credit sales	receipts from other sources

cash book – sample entries of receipts

Study each of the four entries and see how each of them is entered twice.

CASH BOOK – debit side (receipts)				Analysis columns			
Date	Details	Cash	Bank	VAT	Cash sales	Receivables	Other income
20XX		£	£	£	£	£	£
1 May	J Spiro [1]	120.00		20.00	100.00		
2 May	AXO Limited [2]		500.00			500.00	
3 May	RBL Limited [3]		100.00			100.00	
4 May	T Ennant [4]		340.00				340.00

[1] Receipt of £120 cash for goods sold. VAT of £20 is listed separately and deducted from £120 to produce a cash sales figure of £100.

[2] £500 received from a credit customer. VAT is not deducted or listed separately.

[3] £100 received from a credit customer. VAT is not deducted or listed separately.

[4] £340 payment received for rent for office space (other income). No VAT has been charged.

money paid out – analysed cash book (credit side)

As with the debit side, each transaction is recorded **twice**, firstly in a left-hand column, and then **again** in the appropriate **right-hand** analysis column(s).

The columns of a credit side of a cash book are explained in the diagram below, and an example with sample entries is set out on the next page with explanatory notes.

CASH BOOK – credit side (payments)				Analysis columns			
Date	Details	Cash	Bank	VAT	Cash purchases	Payables	Other expenses
		£	£	£	£	£	£

date of the entry	details of the entry	payments	VAT	cash purchases less VAT	payments for credit purchases	payments for other expenses

cash book – sample entries of payments (credit side)

Study each of the four entries and see how each of them is entered twice.

CASH BOOK – credit side (payments)				Analysis columns			
Date	Details	Cash	Bank	VAT	Cash purchases	Payables	Other expenses
20XX		£	£	£	£	£	£
1 May	Zip Supplies [1]	240.00		40.00	200.00		
2 May	P Ringel [2]		450.00			450.00	
3 May	S Marty [3]		150.00			150.00	
4 May	INS Limited [4]		680.00				680.00

[1] £240 cash payment for goods sold. VAT of £40 is listed separately and deducted from £240 to produce a cash purchases figure of £200.

[2] £450 paid to a credit supplier. VAT is not deducted or listed separately.

[3] £150 paid to a credit supplier. VAT is not deducted or listed separately.

[4] £680 payment for insurance. VAT has not been charged.

introduction to bookkeeping wise guide – cash book – introduction

15 Balancing the cash book

It is assumed that you already know how double-entry works and how accounts are balanced.

This Section now takes you through the totalling up of the cash book columns and shows you how to balance the Cash and Bank accounts.

why balance the cash book?

The purpose of balancing the cash book at regular intervals (eg weekly) is:

▨ to calculate the **balance of Cash account** – this is the amount of cash held by the business, excluding any petty cash

▨ to calculate the **balance of Bank account** – this is the amount the business reckons it has in its bank account

▨ to total up and transfer amounts from the analysis columns

stage 1 – totalling the columns and balancing the accounts

The cash book debit side with sample entries has been expanded on this page to show:

- the opening balances of **Cash account** and **Bank account** – these represent the amount of cash held and the bank balance of the business as shown in the cash book for the previous period (these are the figures in the dotted frame box)
- the totals of all the money columns (the figures in the solid frame box)

The cash book credit side is on the next page and is needed to balance the accounts.

CASH BOOK – debit side (receipts)				Analysis columns			
Date	Details	Cash	Bank	VAT	Cash sales	Receivables	Other income
20XX		£	£	£	£	£	£
1 May	Balance b/d	390.00	485.00				
1 May	J Spiro	120.00		20.00	100.00		
2 May	AXO Limited		500.00			500.00	
3 May	RBL Limited		100.00			100.00	
4 May	T Ennant		340.00				340.00
		510.00	1,425.00	20.00	100.00	600.00	340.00

introduction to bookkeeping wise guide – balancing the cash book

CASH BOOK – credit side (payments)				Analysis columns			
Date	Details	Cash	Bank	VAT	Cash purchases	Payables	Other expenses
20XX		£	£	£	£	£	£
1 May	Zip Supplies	240.00		40.00	200.00		
2 May	P Ringel		450.00			450.00	
3 May	S Marty		150.00			150.00	
4 May	INS Limited		680.00				680.00
		510.00	1,425.00	40.00	200.00	600.00	680.00

You are now half way through the balancing procedure:

▨ the columns have been added up

▨ totals have all been written on the bottom line

▨ **BUT** the cash and bank totals on the credit side (in the dotted frame box) are the totals copied from the **debit side columns** of the cash book shown on the previous page, as these are **higher** than the credit side totals (which are not written in the cash book)

- Balancing figures can now be calculated as follows and noted down:
  — cash account: £510 (higher total) minus lower total (£240) = £270 (debit balance)
  — bank account: £1,425 (higher total) minus lower total (£1,280) = £145 (debit balance)
- Insert the cash and bank balancing figures (£270 and £145) as shown below:
  — on the **credit** side **above** the totals line with the day date and 'Balances c/d'
  — on the **debit** side **below** the totals line with the **next** day date and 'Balances b/d'

| CASH BOOK – debit side (receipts) ||||
Date	Details	Cash	Bank
20XX		£	£
1 May	Balance b/d	390.00	485.00
1 May	J Spiro	120.00	
2 May	AXO Limited		500.00
3 May	RBL Limited		100.00
4 May	T Ennant		340.00
		510.00	1,425.00
5 May	Balances b/d	270.00	145.00

| CASH BOOK – credit side (payments) ||||
Date	Details	Cash	Bank
20XX		£	£
1 May	Zip Supplies	240.00	
2 May	P Ringel		450.00
3 May	S Marty		150.00
4 May	INS Limited		680.00
4 May	Balances c/d	270.00	145.00
		510.00	1,425.00

introduction to bookkeeping wise guide – balancing the cash book

cash book – some further things to look out for

▨ **Bank account**   When the cash book is balanced, the **balance** of Bank account can end up either on the debit side or on the credit side:

debit balance = money in the bank (think: an asset = a debit)

credit balance = bank overdraft (think: a liability = a credit)

NOTE! On a bank statement, it's the other way round – an overdraft is a debit balance and money in the account a credit balance. This is because the statement, an essential check on cash book accuracy, is presented from the bank's point of view.

▨ **Cash account**   The balance of Cash account is always a **debit balance** (an asset) – if you think about it, you cannot have negative cash.

▨ **VAT**   **The golden rule is that the only VAT shown in the cash book is VAT on cash purchases and cash sales.**

The reason for this is that VAT on credit sales and purchases has already been recorded from invoices and credit notes into the day books and then in the ledgers.

The **totals** of the VAT columns in the cash book are transferred to VAT account as follows:

— cash book receipts total (debit side) is credited to VAT account
— cash book payments total (credit side) is debited to VAT account

16 Cash book to ledger accounts

CASH BOOK – A BOOK OF PRIME ENTRY

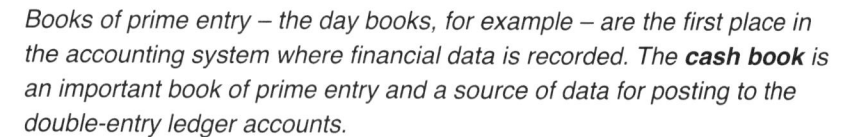

*Books of prime entry – the day books, for example – are the first place in the accounting system where financial data is recorded. The **cash book** is an important book of prime entry and a source of data for posting to the double-entry ledger accounts.*

The **cash book** incorporates two double-entry accounts which record:
— cash (notes and coins) received and paid out – this is **cash account**
— incoming bank payments and outgoing bank payments – this is **bank account**

▮ The cash book records:
— **money in** on **the left** – these are **debits**
— **money out** on **the right** – these are **credits**

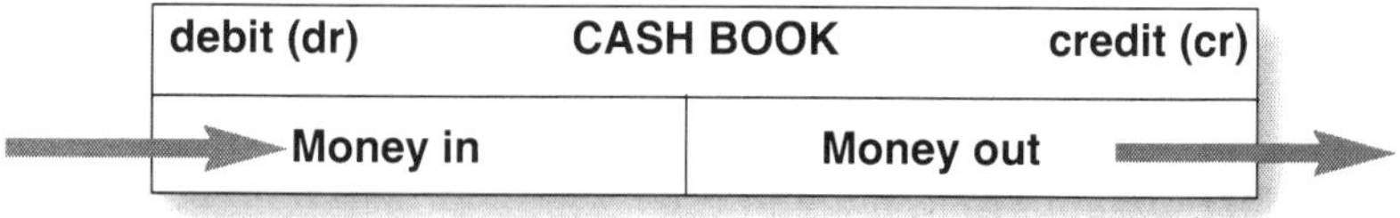

debit (dr)	CASH BOOK	credit (cr)
Money in		Money out

how to work out the debits and credits for cash book transactions

- If the transaction is a **receipt** (money in), the entry in the cash book will be a **debit** and so **the other entry will be a credit** – for example, to the account of a customer who has paid an invoice, or for cash received from cash sales.
- If the transaction is a **payment** (money out), the entry in the cash book will be a **credit** and so **the other entry will be a debit** – for example, to the account of a supplier who has been sent a payment, or cash used to pay for expenses.

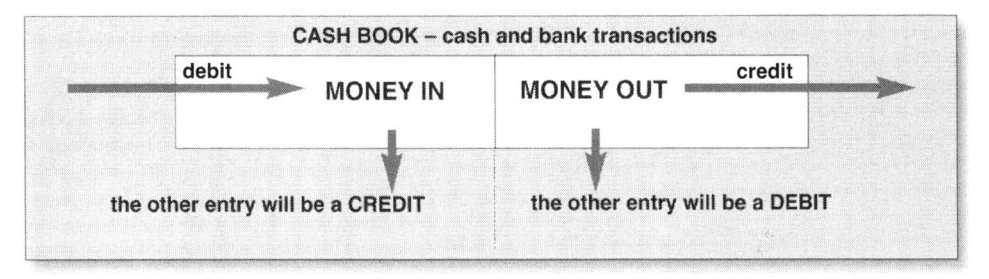

CASH BOOK – cash and bank transactions

debit → MONEY IN	MONEY OUT → credit
the other entry will be a CREDIT	the other entry will be a DEBIT

*If you need further help with **debits and credits** in double-entry, please see pages 11-13.*

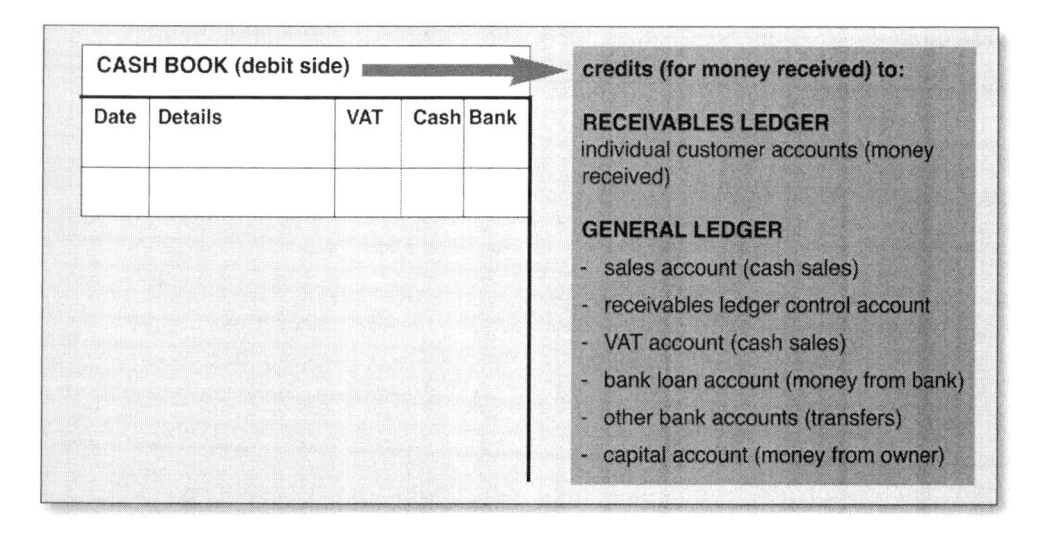

double-entry from the cash book receipts (left-hand) side

The diagram below shows examples of the **credit** account entries which are made to complete the double-entry from the **debit** side of the cash book.

CASH BOOK (debit side)					credits (for money received) to:

Date	Details	VAT	Cash	Bank

credits (for money received) to:

RECEIVABLES LEDGER
individual customer accounts (money received)

GENERAL LEDGER

- sales account (cash sales)

- receivables ledger control account

- VAT account (cash sales)

- bank loan account (money from bank)

- other bank accounts (transfers)

- capital account (money from owner)

double-entry from the cash book payments (right-hand) side

The diagram below shows examples of the **debit** account entries which are made to complete the double-entry from the **credit** side of the cash book.

debits (for money paid out) to:	CASH BOOK (credit side)			
PAYABLES LEDGER individual supplier accounts (money paid) **GENERAL LEDGER** - purchases account (cash purchases) - payables ledger control account - VAT account (cash purchases only) - bank loan account (loan repayments) - other bank accounts (transfers) - drawings account (money taken out by the owners) - expense accounts - purchase of assets	Date	Details	VAT	Cash	Bank

cash book – points to watch out for

■ **Is the bank or cash account contained in the cash book?**

In this Wise Guide, the bank or cash accounts shown in the cash book are the actual **double-entry accounts** belonging to the general ledger. In this case, these accounts do not need posting to the ledgers.

Sometimes the bank or cash accounts contained in the cash book are not double-entry accounts and need to be posted to **separate bank or cash control accounts in the general ledger**. In this case, the cash book is used only as a **book of prime entry**.

■ **Cash transactions only in the VAT columns**

Remember that the entries in the VAT columns relate to cash sales or purchases only. These are posted to the VAT account from the cash book.

VAT on credit sales and credit purchases **has already been posted to the ledger accounts through the day books**.

■ Differing formats – the use of extra analysis columns

There are many different cash book formats, so it is important to remember that the format shown in this Wise Guide is not the one and only correct way to organise a cash book.

cash book – summary

The diagram shown below is central to an understanding of the cash book. Memorise it.

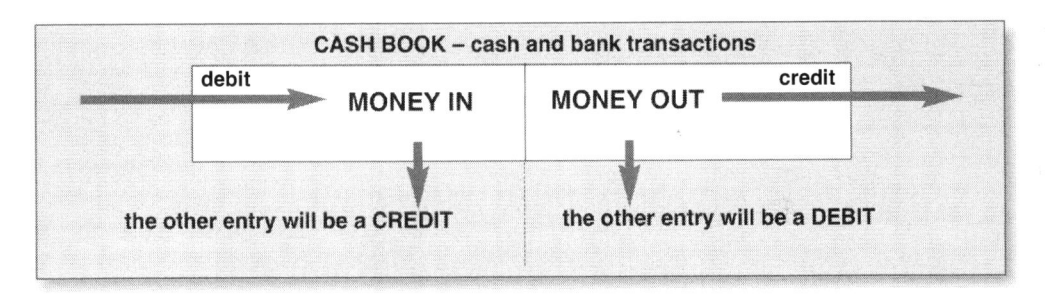

```
CASH BOOK – cash and bank transactions
    debit                                              credit
    ──────▶  MONEY IN    │    MONEY OUT  ──────▶
                │                    │
                ▼                    ▼
    the other entry will be a CREDIT    the other entry will be a DEBIT
```

17 Petty cash book

PETTY CASH BOOK – WHAT IT IS FOR

*A **petty cash book** records small cash payments for purchases and expenses, eg stationery, postage and taxi fares.*

*A petty cash book can be a **book of prime entry** for posting to the double-entry ledger accounts and can **sometimes** contain the **petty cash account**.*

the petty cash procedure

- **Petty cash** is a small store of notes and coins – up to £100, for example – kept in a locked tin and looked after by the **petty cashier**.

- An employee making a small cash purchase fills in a **petty cash voucher** with the details of the purchase and attaches the receipt to the petty cash voucher.

- The employee signs the voucher and the petty cashier checks all the details.

- The petty cashier signs and authorises the voucher if the amount is within the authorisation limit and gives the person the cash from the petty cash box; if the amount is higher than the limit, a manager may need to sign the voucher.

■ The **petty cash voucher** details entered into the **petty cash book** are shown below:

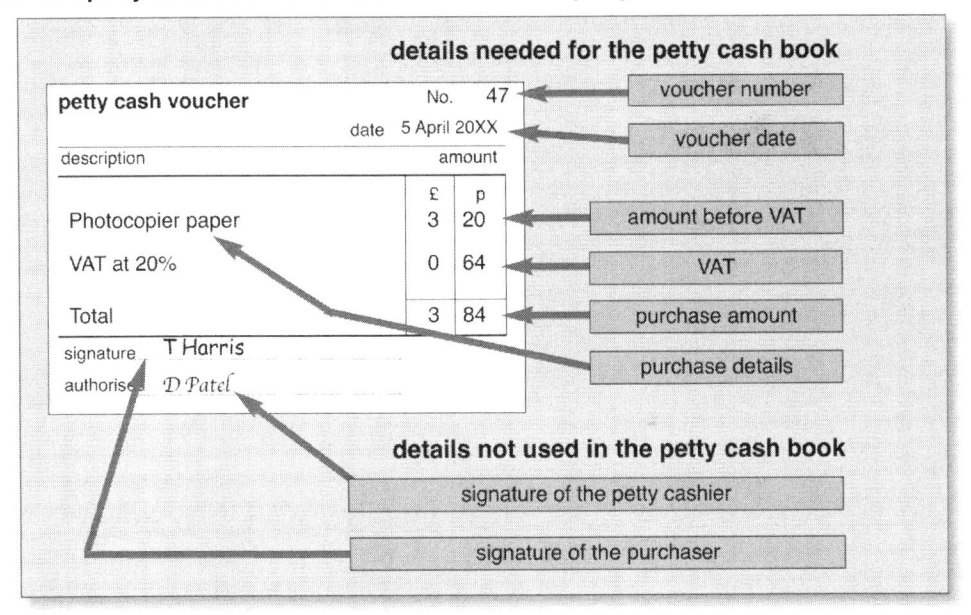

details needed for the petty cash book

petty cash voucher		No.	47	← voucher number
	date	5 April 20XX		← voucher date

description	amount	
	£	p
Photocopier paper	3	20	← amount before VAT
VAT at 20%	0	64	← VAT
Total	3	84	← purchase amount

← purchase details

signature T Harris
authorised D Patel

details not used in the petty cash book

signature of the petty cashier

signature of the purchaser

introduction to bookkeeping wise guide – petty cash book

authorisation of petty cash

Payment out of petty cash is normally only allowed if:

▨   it is authorised by the petty cashier or manager – who need to sign the voucher

▨   it is on the list of items authorised by the business – for example, stationery, taxi fares, cleaning materials, refreshments for clients, postage stamps

▨   it is within the authorisation limit per transaction set by the business, eg £25

calculation of VAT on petty cash vouchers

▨   VAT on a petty cash purchase needs to be accounted for.

▨   VAT is recorded on a petty cash voucher from the receipt (see previous page).

▨   VAT is calculated using the following formula:

Purchase amount before VAT $\times \dfrac{VAT\ rate}{100} = VAT\ amount$

For example: £8.00 $\times$ $20/_{100}$ = £1.60 (VAT amount)

Therefore, the total amount will be £8.00 + £1.60 = £9.60.

BUT, if only the whole total is shown, the VAT amount will have to be calculated. See the next page.

petty cash voucher – working out the missing VAT

Suppose you are asked to prepare a petty cash voucher but find that the receipt does not show the VAT amount but only the whole total. You will need to work out the figures for the VAT and the amount before VAT is added on.

petty cash voucher		No. 105
	date	5 April 20XX
description		amount
	£	p
Suspension files	?	??
VAT at 20%	?	??
Total	12	00
signature		
authorised		

You can use a formula or use what is known as the 'VAT fraction' to work out the VAT content with VAT at 20%.

The **formula** for finding out the price **before VAT is added on** is:

$$\text{total amount paid} \times \frac{100}{100 + \text{VAT rate}} \quad \ldots \text{in this case} \ldots \quad £12 \times \frac{100}{100 + 20} = \frac{£1,200}{120} = £10$$

Alternatively, you can apply the **VAT fraction** of $1/6$ to work out the **VAT content** of £12, ie £12 × $\frac{1}{6}$ = £2 VAT ... or even more easily ... divide the £12 by 6 = £2 VAT.

introduction to bookkeeping wise guide – petty cash book

topping up the petty cash

- From time to time – eg every week – the petty cash box will need topping up.

- Normally a 'top limit' of cash is specified so that each time, it will be topped up to this limit, say £100, by the cashier.

- This top limit is known as the 'imprest' amount.

- It follows that the amount of the top up will always be the same as the amount spent since the last top up. It is like topping up the fuel tank of a car until it is full – the amount of fuel you put in will be the same as the amount that you have used.

- The calculation is:

	Petty cash held after top up at the start of the week	£100.00
minus	Petty cash payments out during the week	£75.00
equals	Petty cash in the tin at the end of the week	£25.00
plus	Top up of cash to imprest amount	£75.00
equals	Cash at start of the next week	£100.00

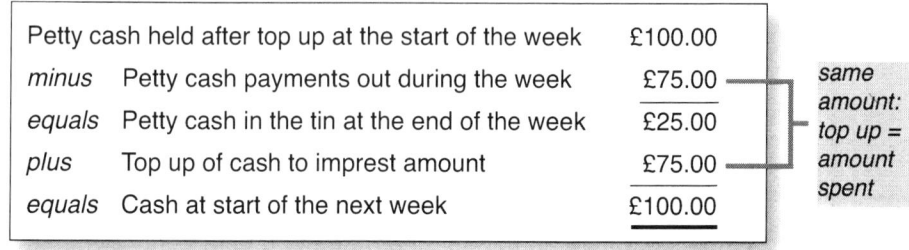

same amount: top up = amount spent

getting the cash for the petty cash top up

- Topping up the petty cash is known as **petty cash reimbursement**.
- The cash is normally obtained by making a cash withdrawal from the bank account for the 'top up' amount.
- In order to obtain this cash, the petty cashier can request a cash withdrawal from a more senior member of the accounting staff on a **cash requisition form**.

CASH REQUISITION FORM	
Amount	£75
Date	5 Feb 20XX
Details	Petty cash reimbursement
Signature	H Anslow, petty cashier
Authorised	S Khan, accounts supervisor

petty cash book layout

- The petty cash book is in two halves; the right-hand half provides an analysis of the payments listed in the 'Total payments' column in the left-hand half.
- The left-hand side contains the petty cash account:
  - the **receipts** column is the **debit** side; the balance b/d of £100 is the amount of cash in petty cash after it has been topped up (the 'imprest' amount). The b/d balance on the petty cash account will always be on the debit side. It is not possible to 'overdraw' cash.
  - the **total payments** column is the **credit** side, showing petty cash payments made
- There are two payments listed:
  - a £12 payment for pens (analysed into VAT of £2 and £10 stationery)
  - a £9.60 payment for a taxi fare (analysed into VAT of £1.60 and £8.00 travel)

debit				credit				
Receipts	Date	Details	Voucher number	Total payments	Analysis columns			
					VAT	Postage	Travel	Stationery
100.00	1 Feb	Bal b/d						
	1 Feb	Pens	456	12.00	2.00			10.00
	2 Feb	Taxi	457	9.60	1.60		8.00	

writing up and totalling the petty cash book

- The petty cash book starts on 1 February with a balance of £100 cash held.
- Payments are then recorded from the petty cash vouchers – the total of each payment is recorded in the Total payments column. It is also entered in the analysis columns with the VAT shown separately when VAT is included in the payment.
- There is no VAT on postage stamps and so none is recorded in the VAT column.
- The columns are added up. Note that the analysis totals add up to the total payment.

\multicolumn{4}{c	}{debit}	\multicolumn{5}{c}{credit}
Receipts	Date	Details	Voucher number	Total payments	\multicolumn{4}{c}{Analysis columns}
					VAT	Postage	Travel	Stationery
100.00	1 Feb	Bal b/d						
	1 Feb	Pens	456	12.00	2.00			10.00
	2 Feb	Taxi	457	9.60	1.60		8.00	
	3 Feb	Stamps	458	17.50		17.50		
	4 Feb	Folders	459	24.00	4.00			20.00
				63.10	7.60	17.50	8.00	30.00

these totals added up should equal £63.10

introduction to bookkeeping wise guide – petty cash book

balancing the petty cash book

- On 5 February the petty cash has received a top up of £63.10 to bring the petty cash total up to £100.00. This £63.10 is recorded in the Receipts column.
- The petty cash book is then balanced using the Receipts and Payments columns. The total is £163.10 and the balance c/d and b/d is £100, the amount of cash held.

debit				credit				
Receipts	Date	Details	Voucher number	Total payments	Analysis columns			
					VAT	Postage	Travel	Stationery
100.00	1 Feb	Bal b/d						
	1 Feb	Pens	456	12.00	2.00			10.00
	2 Feb	Taxi	457	9.60	1.60		8.00	
top up of cash	3 Feb	Stamps	458	17.50		17.50		
	4 Feb	Folders	459	24.00	4.00			20.00
↓				63.10	7.60	17.50	8.00	30.00
63.10	5 Feb	Bank						
	5 Feb	Bal c/d		100.00				
163.10	*balance of cash*			163.10				
100.00	6 Feb	Bal b/d						

counting and agreeing the petty cash

- It is important to check regularly the amount of cash held in the petty cash box with the total recorded in the petty cash book – to detect errors or, even worse, theft.
- A **cash analysis form** (shown on the right) is used to list the notes and coins and calculate the total cash held.
- Any discrepancy between the balance of cash in the petty cash book and the actual cash held should be investigated.
- Checking is often done when the petty cash book has been balanced and the petty cash box has been topped up to the imprest amount.
- If a surprise check is done at any other time, the total cash should be:

  *imprest (topped up) amount **minus** the total of payments made since the top up (ie the total of all petty cash vouchers issued since the top up).*

Notes & coins	Number	Value (£)
£20 notes	1	20.00
£10 notes	1	10.00
£5 notes	3	15.00
£2 coins	1	2.00
£1 coins	7	7.00
50p coins	4	2.00
20p coins	8	1.60
10p coins	5	0.50
5p coins	4	0.20
2p coins	7	0.14
1p coins	6	0.06
TOTAL		**58.50**

18 Petty cash book to ledger accounts

Petty cash book - how it fits into the accounting system

*A **petty cash book** records small cash payments for purchases and expenses, eg stationery, postage and taxi fares.*

*A petty cash book can also be a book of **prime entry** and a source of data for posting to the double-entry ledger accounts.*

the petty cash procedure

- **Petty cash** is a small store of notes and coins – up to £100 for example – kept in a locked tin and looked after by the **petty cashier**.

- Someone making a small cash purchase fills in a **petty cash voucher** with the details of the purchase, attaches the receipt to the petty cash voucher and signs it.

- The petty cashier checks all the details, the voucher is authorised and signed and the person is given the cash from the petty cash box.

- The relevant details on the petty cash voucher are then recorded by the petty cashier in a **petty cash book** — see pages 86-88 for a typical layout.

petty cash book – recording transactions

The petty cash book:

- has a **debit** side for **cash paid in** when the petty cash box is topped up
- has a **credit** side for **cash paid out**

debit (dr)	PETTY CASH BOOK	credit (cr)
Cash in (top up)		Cash out (expenses)

- the **credit side** records the details from the petty cash vouchers:
  - the date and the **total** amount of each voucher
  - the details of what has been bought, eg postage stamps, cleaning materials
  - the **VAT** content of the voucher
  - the **'net'** amount of the voucher (before VAT) in the correct analysis column, eg 'Postage', Office expenses, Stationery, Fuel etc
- the Amount, VAT and analysis columns are then all added up
- all the totals are checked by 'cross casting' – as you would in a day book

petty cash book – its place in the accounting system

The petty cash book can be a **book of prime entry**:

▧   it is the main source from which details are taken to make entries in the ledgers

▧   in this case, the general ledger will include a **petty cash control account** to summarise payments in and out of petty cash

Note: the petty cash book can sometimes incorporate the double-entry petty cash account (General Ledger), but in this example it is purely a book of prime entry.

Using the petty cash book shown on the next page, the double-entry postings are:

▧ **receipt of cash**	**debit**	Petty cash control account	£100.00
	credit	Bank account	£100.00
▧ **petty cash payments**	using the credit side **totals** as follows:		
	debit	VAT account	£7.00
	debit	Postage account	£26.00
	debit	Office expenses account	£35.00
			£68.00
and then . . .			
	credit	Petty cash control account	£68.00

PETTY CASH BOOK LAYOUT (used as a book of prime entry)

Cash receipts 'in' (debit side)				Cash payments 'out' (credit side) — with analysis columns				
Date 20XX	Details	Voucher Number	Amount	Date 20XX	Details	Amount	VAT	Postage	Office expenses
1 Jul	Balance b/d		100.00						
		52		1 Jul	Postage stamps	26.00		26.00	
		53		4 Jul	Coffee & tea	14.40	2.40		12.00
		54		5 Jul	Thick bleach	3.60	0.60		3.00
				5 Jul	Copy paper	24.00	4.00		20.00
						68.00	7.00	26.00	35.00

GENERAL LEDGER
Note: as this £100 is a **balance b/d**, 'top ups' of cash will have taken place before 1 July.
In each case the entries will have been:
debit Petty cash control account
credit Bank account

GENERAL LEDGER
credit Petty cash control account £68.00

GENERAL LEDGER
debit VAT account £7.00

GENERAL LEDGER
debit Postage account £26.00

GENERAL LEDGER
debit Office expenses account £35.00

introduction to bookkeeping wise guide – petty cash book to ledger accounts

19 The trial balance

HOW ACCURATE IS THE DOUBLE-ENTRY?

Accuracy is important in any accounting system and businesses will use a number of checking processes to avoid mistakes.

Double-entry always requires debits to equal credits. This can be checked by adding up all the debit balances and all the credit balances in the general ledger and **making sure the two totals are the same**.

*This is known as the **trial balance**.*

the trial balance

- Lists all the general ledger account balances at a specific date (eg the last day in the month) in two columns and adds them both up.

- The left-hand column contains the debit balances and the right-hand column. contains the credit balances

- The two totals *should* agree.

EXAMPLE: TRIAL BALANCE

In the example here, a simple trial balance for ABC Ltd is drawn up on 31 May from the account balances shown on the left.

Account name	Balance (£)
Bank (cash at bank)	2,000
Capital	20,000
Electricity	395
Insurance	935
Machinery	4,900
Payables	2,700
Purchases	49,970
Receivables	3,500
Sales	81,000
VAT (payable to HMRC)	870
Wages	42,870

ABC LTD TRIAL BALANCE AS AT 31 MAY

	Debit (£)	Credit (£)
	2,000	
		20,000
	395	
	935	
	4,900	
		2,700
	49,970	
	3,500	
		81,000
		870
	42,870	
Total	104,570	104,570

introduction to bookkeeping wise guide – the trial balance

the purpose of the trial balance

■ Provides a regular check of the arithmetical accuracy of double-entry – any difference in the column totals must be investigated and the error/s corrected.

■ A trial balance is not a guarantee of error-free bookkeeping because transactions may be omitted, duplicated or values entered incorrectly – such errors would not be revealed by the trial balance.

■ The figures in the trial balance are used to produce **financial statements**:

1. the **statement of profit or loss** – a summary of revenue income and expenses that shows how profitable the business is in an accounting period

2. the **statement of financial position** – a summary of assets, liabilities and capital (what the business owns, what it owes and how it is financed) on a given date

importance of accurate entry of transactions – some reasons why it matters

- Whether shown by the trial balance or not, incorrect entry of transactions, including omissions, duplications and value errors, may result in the business owner(s) basing decisions on incorrect information.
- An entry made in the wrong ledger account, eg wrong customer or supplier, may result in customer statement errors or supplier payment errors.
- A date error in a digital system may result in figures being reported in the wrong period.

20 Digital Bookkeeping

Using a computer program for bookkeeping, though based on manual bookkeeping principles, has many advantages over a manual system.

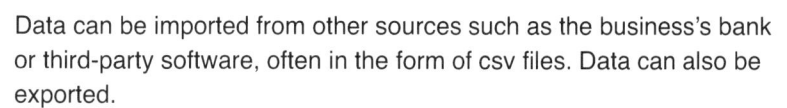

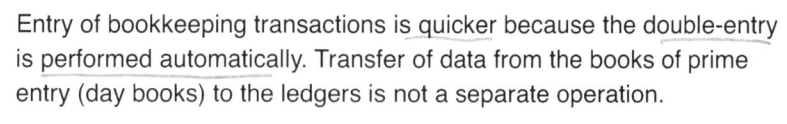

- Data can be imported from other sources such as the business's bank or third-party software, often in the form of csv files. Data can also be exported.

- Entry of bookkeeping transactions is quicker because the double-entry is performed automatically. Transfer of data from the books of prime entry (day books) to the ledgers is not a separate operation.

- Sales invoices can be produced within the program and data automatically transferred to the day book and receivables ledger. Documents including customer statements can be produced and emailed directly from the program.

- Control accounts and subsidiary accounts (receivables and payables ledger accounts) are updated at the same time so are automatically reconciled.

- All balancing operations that would take time in a manual system are done automatically. The trial balance always balances.
- Recurring entries (regular payments or receipts for the same value that happen on the same date in each accounting period) are processed automatically on the date set.
- A range of reports (printouts) is instantly available, eg receivables and payables account balances, bank receipts and payments, Trial Balance.
- The potential for errors is reduced because inputting a transaction is single-entry.

But beware, errors are still possible in a digital system:

- An entry may be completely omitted.
- A transaction may be entered twice, eg where an automatic recurring entry is also entered manually.
- Entries may be entered incorrectly, eg wrong date, wrong values, wrong customer or supplier, wrong general ledger account.

21 Memory aids

KEEPING YOUR MEMORY FIT

The human brain is an odd organ – you can remember the most useless facts, but when it comes to complex matters such as accounting procedures the mind can go completely blank. But it is possible to train your brain.

At the beginning of this Guide there are some revision tips which suggest that you can study effectively and recall information by . . .

- **Observing**, ie remembering what information looks like on the page, using diagrams, lists, mind-maps and colour coding. Memory is very visual.

- **Writing** information down, using flash cards, post-it notes, notes on a phone. It is the actual process of writing which helps to fix the information in the brain.

- **Learning** by regularly going through your course notes and textbooks. Find a 'study buddy' in your class (or online) to teach and test each other as the course progresses.

- **Chill out** when you get tired. Give your brain a chance to recover. Get some exercise and fresh air, work out. In the ancient world there was the saying that a fit body is usually home to a fit mind.

- **Treats** – promise yourself rewards when you have finished studying; meet friends, eat chocolate, have a drink, listen to music.

exam preparation

- **Practise, practise, practise** when preparing for your assessment.

  Practise the questions and assessments in the Osborne Books workbooks.

some aids to memory

Below are blank spaces for you to set out ways of remembering debit and credit entries.

Double-entry – on which side does the entry go? Make a list on the T account format below of what type of accounts are normally debits and which are normally credits, eg purchases, sales, liabilities, assets, capital, drawings etc.

debits	credits
Assets	Liabilities
Drawings	income
Expense	Capital
purchase	sales

Accounting equation – write down the accounting equation formula in the gap below.

$A - L = C$

Jot down some examples of the different elements of the equation.

Assets	
Liabilities	
Capital	

introduction to bookkeeping wise guide – memory aids

Index

Account reconciliation, 57-61
Accounting equation, 14-19
Accounting process, 6-7
Assets, 14-20

Balancing accounts, 23-26
Bank account, 62,68,72,74,78
Books of prime entry, 7,44,74
Bulk discount, 38

Capital, 14-19
Capital and revenue, 20-22
Capital expense, 21
Capital income, 22

Cash book,
    analysed cash book, 64-67
    balancing, 68-73
    entries to ledger accounts, 74-79
    introduction to, 62-67
Coding, 35
Credit note, 32

Day books, 44-56
Digital bookkeeping, 98-99
Discounts, 38-43
Double-entry, 8-13
Double-entry and cash book, 74-79
Double-entry and petty cash book, 90-93

Double-entry principles, 8-13
Double-entry rules, 10

Financial documents, 27-35, 36-37

General ledger, 49-54, 76-78, 92-93

Invoice, 28, 31
Invoice calculations, 37

Liabilities, 14-19

Payables, 13, 63, 66-67
Payables ledger, 52-54
Petty cash book, 80-93
    balancing, 88
    cash analysis, 89
    entries to ledger accounts, 90-93
    imprest, 84
    layout, 86
    top-up, 84
    writing up, 87
Petty cash voucher, 81
Prompt payment discount, 39, 43, 55-56
Purchases day book, 45-46
Purchases returns day book, 45-46

Quotation, 28

Receivables, 12, 63, 64-65
Receivables ledger, 49-51
Reconciliation of accounts, 57-61

Remittance advice, 34
Revenue expense, 21
Revenue income, 22

Sales day book, 45-50
Sales returns day book, 45-51
Statement of account, 33,57-61
Statement of financial position, 96
Statement of profit or loss, 96

'T' accounts, 8-9
Trade discount, 38-40
Trial balance, 94-96

VAT, 31,32,36,41-43
VAT and prompt payment discount, 43
VAT calculation, 41
VAT rounding, 42